CONFLICT, CONFLICT RESOLUTION & MEDIATION

Theory, Process & Practice

Clay Phillips

WHY THE CHESSBOARD COVER?

In my first book *Getting Started as a Mediator: The Seven Steps for Starting and Building a Successful Mediation Practice* I began to explain some of the similarities between chess and the *human conflict condition*, primarily the consequence effect of the decisions we make. Each chess piece has a specific purpose, role, capabilities and limitations. The strategy of the chess master involves more than learning and understanding the traits of each piece he also considers and anticipates the opportunities that each consequence will create. Within the human conflict condition, we are constantly planning – constantly considering and processing information that ultimately leads to a decision. What chess teaches us about our day-to-day interactions with ourselves and others is two-fold: as long as we consider those around us and our surroundings, we will always have more opportunities than problems; and, even when we don't or refuse to make a decision, we made a decision… to not decide. No one gets a break. Chess and the human conflict condition are both centered on *decisions* and *consequences,* except chess allows a limited amount of time for critical thought and strategic planning.

Copyright © 2017. Clay Phillips. All rights reserved.
ClayPhillipsBooks.com

ISBN-13: 978-0-9992723-1-2

Conflict is a natural and healthy part of our lives, but it usually isn't perceived that way. To appreciate conflict as it presents itself, we must first understand its purpose. In a nutshell, conflict exists as a result of a decision we made or were involved in making - directly or indirectly - particularly when our decisions are concerning a solution. What we do between the conflict and the solution - the decision-making - is the real purpose of conflict. The opportunity to make better decisions in the future. This book describes and details the origins of human conflict (intrapersonal, interpersonal, and extra personal) by examining and illustrating how it affects and is affected by our systems of belief, emotion, and behavior. In this volume, I share my diagrams of these experiences in the Phillips Interpersonal Conflict Condition Model in hopes of providing a better understanding of how and why we experience conflict, how we process and go about resolving the conflict, and how mediation works to that end. This book is not just for mediators and attorneys. Anyone can benefit from a better understanding of this topic.

DEDICATION

This book, Volume 1 of The Mediator's Guidebook is dedicated to my lovely and wonderful wife, Deborah. She inspires me, believes in me even when I don't, brainstorms with me, reality-checks me, tolerates my creativity, seems to appreciate my spontaneity, embraces my attention deficit, and shows me every day what an honorable person looks like. You are the best part of my life, Baby.

CONTENTS

1. THE HUMAN CONFLICT CONDITION	1
Intrapersonal Conflict.	2
Interpersonal Conflict.	6
Extrapersonal Conflict.	10
2. DIMENSIONS OF THE HUMAN CONDITION	12
The Cognitive Dimension.	17
The Emotional Dimension.	21
The Behavioral Dimension.	29
3. PIpCC	35
Triangles.	36
Dots… or not?	42
Blobs.	54
4. CONFLICT RESOLUTION & MEDIATION	58
Integrity.	63
Impartiality.	68
Mutual Respect.	75
ABOUT THE AUTHOR	79

1. THE HUMAN CONFLICT CONDITION

Every conflict we humans are involved with/in is a direct or indirect result of a decision we made at some point in time. Now, before you take exception to that statement, I'll ask you to entertain this perspective... the perspective that, while we each do not experience conflict for the same reasons, we do experience conflict in the same ways. In the broader sense, we experience conflict in three fundamental regions of our being: conflict within and about ourselves *(intrapersonal)*; conflict with and about others *(interpersonal)*; and, conflict with our external environment and surroundings, minus other people *(extrapersonal)*. With this perspective, we can better understand the origin of conflict, how it affects us, why we react to conflict in different ways, how our reactions and resulting behavior impacts us, those around us and our surroundings, and how the noise of the outside world factors into human conflict, human conflict resolution, and human conflict management... or, as I have coined it, the *human conflict condition*. Keep in mind, I'm a mediator, not a mental health professional and that this is only a mediator's perspective.

Intrapersonal Conflict.

So, let's start with the precise moment you woke up this morning. From that point forward, list what you did, as the events occurred. To keep this example simple, just write down the first ten:

1. I awoke.
2. _____.
3. _____.
4. _____.
5. _____.
6. _____.
7. _____.
8. _____.
9. _____.
10. _____.

Now, beside each of your responses *(to the left of the numeral for each response)* write whether this occurrence was *involuntary* or *voluntary*. For example, breathing and having a pulse are *involuntary*. Also, some of us awaken every day without the need for an alarm clock - we just *wake up at the same time* every day. Some people call this their *internal clock* and most would likely refer to it as involuntary. Actually, this is an example of *trained* or *conditioned* behavior *(which makes it a hybrid of involuntary and voluntary)*. So, go ahead and label each of your responses now.

Your responses might look something like mine:
1. I awoke.
2. I hit the snooze button.
3. I awoke again.
4. I hit the snooze button again.
5. I turned on the TV and watched the morning news.
6. I got out of bed and went to the bathroom.
7. I washed my face and hands.
8. I went into the kitchen and got something to eat and drink.
9. I took a shower.
10. I brushed my teeth.

In this example, I have depicted what most mornings look like for me from the time I awake until the time I am dressed. Now, when I assign whether each was involuntary (I), voluntary (V) or a hybrid (I/V), it will look like this:

I/V 1. I awoke.
V   2. I hit the snooze button.
I/V 3. I awoke again.
V   4. I hit the snooze button again, but stayed awake.
V   5. I turned on the TV and watched the morning news.
V   6. I got out of bed and went to the bathroom.
V   7. I washed my face and hands.

V 8. I went into the kitchen and got something to eat and drink.
V 9. I took a shower.
V 10. I brushed my teeth

Are you seeing a theme taking shape yet? Add the next ten occurrences in your day, if you like. Mine would look something like this:

V 11. I got dressed.
V 12. I grabbed my bag and headed to the garage.
V 13. I drove to my office.
V 14. I put my things down in my office.
V 15. I went to the restroom.
V 16. I got a cup of coffee.
V 17. I read and responded to emails.
V 18. I made a few phone calls.
V 19. I got another cup of coffee.

Seeing it yet? After *I* awoke, the occurrences in my day became more and more voluntary. So, *voluntary* in this context means I *decided* to make or allow this event to occur. Conversely, I could have *decided* to *not* get out of bed... or *not* to brush my teeth, or *not* go to work. So, why did I decide *to do* these things rather than *not do* them? Generally, because *to do* them best suited/met my *needs, priorities and values* at the moment each of them occurred. Some examples of my *needs* in these decisions might have been that I had to use the bathroom, or I was hungry, or I needed to stretch and get moving. An example of my *priorities* in these decisions might have been using the bathroom before getting a cup of coffee or something to eat. An example of my *values* in these decisions might have been that need to be on time or early at work because *I have a lot to get done today*, or because *I'm up for a promotion and I want to make sure my appearance or arrival time don't reflect negatively on me*, or because *I just want to keep my job*. Our voluntary decisions are motive-driven.

Now, for each of the responses you gave and identified as voluntary, replace "*I*" with "*I decided to*". After you've done this, examine each of your responses and see if you made any more decisions between each of them. For example, in my list (the first ten), between numbers 5 and 6, I could insert "I changed the channel" or more accurately "I *decided to* change channel", or could insert "I turned the volume up/down" or more accurately "I *decided to* turn the volume up/down". How many more "I decided to's" can you insert between each of your *voluntary* responses? You see, so little of our conscious time is comprised of involuntary occurrences. So, most of it is comprised of the *voluntary decisions* we make, or the *result* of our voluntary decisions. When things don't go as we planned or like, *intrapersonal conflict* occurs. When a voluntary decision is difficult to make for any reason, *intrapersonal conflict* occurs. When we second-guess our voluntary decisions - good, bad or indifferent - *intrapersonal conflict* occurs. When we experience shame, guilt or regret, *intrapersonal conflict* occurs. Intrapersonal conflict is rooted in the voluntary decisions we make, and those decisions are made based on our needs, priorities and values at the moment the decision is made. Conflict begins within each of us from the very first voluntary decision we make.

Interpersonal Conflict.

Understanding interpersonal conflict is no less specific and no more complicated than understanding intrapersonal conflict. Look at it this way, the minute you interact with another person at the beginning of your day, inter-personal conflict has begun. Why? Well, it's because now your needs, priorities and values are competing with the needs, priorities and values of that other person. And the next person you meet, and so on. Now, magnify this competition by the number of people you interact with everyday... formally, informally, directly, and indirectly. A great example of this is your commute to work every day, whether it's by car, boat, train or airplane. Who loves sitting on the interstate? How about *that person* that stays in the left lane but hasn't passed another car since they've been there? Does that annoy you? Even a little? What the heck?! Well, just remember how tough a decision it was earlier when you were choosing which shirt or shoes or necktie to wear today.

Now consider that these other people surrounding you on the interstate - or in your car if you carpool - have experienced their own *brew or concoction* of intrapersonal conflict before bumping into you. How'd they sleep last night? How's their marriage? Are they under financial pressure? Do they hate their job? Are they normally grumpy no matter what? Are they just a jerk or some inconsiderate lollygagger that's bent to ruin your day? If any of this sounds familiar it's because each of us has some sort(s) of pressure on us that affects our behavior - particularly around others and more particularly around those closest to us and those we don't know or have never met.

Have you ever had someone say to you *"I understand."*? How about *"I know how you feel."*? Or, *"That's just how I am."*? Whether the person saying these things is sincere or not, what matters most is how you perceive them. Are they really being sincere, or are they placating or patronizing me? Do they really give a flip or are they trying to pacify me until they can leave? The better and most informing question is, *why* do we say these things to each other at all - knowing how it makes us feel when others say them to us? Well, it's simple. So simple that we easily and readily adapt this behavior even though it causes us some internal conflict *(intrapersonal)*. Generally, we say *these things* to each other for a handful of reasons. Here are a few of the most common:

- We believe what we're saying. By comparing their situation to events in our lives, we convince

ourselves that we really do *understand* or *know how they feel* at that moment.
- We feel sorry for the other person. We're just a softy sometimes... or, more times than not... or, usually... OR we're always out looking for someone to feel sorry for or rescue.
- If we don't show them concern or affection, no one else will. We have convinced ourselves that we have superhuman powers that no one else does and something terrible will happen to them or us if we don't get involved *(OK, maybe that's a little extreme... or, maybe not)*.
- We think short answers will make for a short conversation. We're annoyed when someone goes on and on about their life's difficulties so we try to deflect the conversation by showing sympathy - genuinely or not.
- Because we're not paying attention and we don't want them to know. Whether we're busy and can't listen right now or if it's the same person griping about the same old thing, we can fade in and out of the conversation and toss in these phrases when the other person pauses or stops talking.

Now, whether or not any of these responses resonate with you, read them again and see which one(s) of these responses do and do not involve voluntary decision-making. Well, if we're aware that this other person is in our presence and they believe they are having a conversation with us, then all of these responses are voluntary decisions. In other words, we had a choice as to how we would act, react, interact and we chose... we decided. Feeling conflicted right now? Good... you should.

To experience this is to learn it that much better. We'll talk more about where that's coming from and some tricks on how to deal with it as it happens.

We are each walking, talking, breathing, multi-tasking, multi-belief, multi-value, multi-preference, multi-thought, multi-need, multi-want, multi-concern, multi-happiness, multi-sadness, multi-fear, multi-regret, multi-shame, multi-interest, multi-quirk, multi-distraction, unique and magnificent creatures that no one else will ever understand completely. If we believe this - and I do - then why do we have such complicated expectations of each other? Expectations that someone else's *multi's* will align with ours and that they will fall in the same priority. Ready for some good news? Some relief? Read on.

So, we hear countless people referring to psyche, and personality, and culture, and a dozen or more reasons as to why we're different and why we experience conflict with others. The simple truth is that we experience conflict with others *because* we are different, not that we have differences. So, what's the difference? *(pun intended)* The difference is that if we made everyone on the planet the same skin color, the same gender, the same height, the same hair color/texture/length, the same voice, and that's all we changed... we would see that what makes us different - REALLY different - is what's on the inside.

What no one else will never know about us unless 1. we share it with them, and 2. if they choose to believe it.

For the time being, there's your basic formula for the interpersonal relationship: what we share with others and they share with us, and what we choose to believe. I bet you're thinking "and *why* we believe them", right? Nope. But, if you did think that - or something along those lines - you just demonstrated the core of *interpersonal conflict*. Not because we want to know *why* someone does or doesn't do something, but because we answer that question for them. How many times each day?

More good news and relief for you is coming soon, so keep reading. The science behind all of this is historically proven to be accurate and reliable, and it's very simple science that I'm going to cover in the following modules and lessons.

Extrapersonal Conflict.

Extrapersonal conflict completes the personal conflict construct. It is everything else within our environment other than those things familiar to us, normally planned events of our day-to-day life, and things we typically consider to be somewhat in our control. We experience extrapersonal conflict when something new or unexpected happens in our lives. Extrapersonal conflict can be positive, negative, exciting, tragic, anything… because it's new or unexpected. For example, what would your reaction be if you have the winning PowerBall lottery ticket? How about if you found out this morning that your boss recommended you for a promotion and - up until that moment - you didn't think your boss even knew you existed? Have you ever lost a loved one in an automobile accident, or some other unnatural way? Those feelings of joy, confusion, uncertainty, certainty, awe, disappointment, inspiration, anger, sadness, or even misery that were the result of a new or unexpected experience are examples of extrapersonal conflict. Extrapersonal conflict first greets us with a sense of disbelief. *Is this really happening to me?* Then, shortly thereafter, the feelings of joy, confusion, uncertainty, certainty, awe, disappointment, inspiration, anger, sadness and/or misery begin to set in - and sometimes, not so subtly.

So, you see, conflict is all around us and all conflict isn't bad. Our lives begin and end with conflict every day - the minute we awaken, to the minute we fall asleep, from our first decision or choice of the day to the last. Chocolate or Vanilla? No one gets a break... but ain't life great?

2. DIMENSIONS OF THE HUMAN CONDITION

Essentially, there are three dimensions of the human condition: intra-, inter-, and extrapersonal. Combined, they comprise our living experience amid the decisions we make and those that are made for us. In every case, these dimensions involve the same process by which we experience them. Because these experiences within our intra, inter, and extrapersonal lives are driven greatly by our decisions, we'll examine how this decision-making occurs and the conflict that is created.

Not only do we each experience intra, inter and extrapersonal conflict, we tend to experience them in the same process and order. This process/order is comprised of three dimensions: *cognitive*, *emotional*, and *behavioral*. Each separate of each other, but inextricably connected. This *dynamic trio* is a basic representation of each of us, as individuals, and how we know each other and ourselves. Or, as I *believe*... how we *think* we know each other and ourselves.

I'll start by using a diagram of a simple, three story house. I'd like for you to take a piece of paper and draw this house as I describe it. So, first, let's draw a rectangle to represent the ground or first floor with a couple of windows and a door. Label the first floor *Behavioral*. Next, let's draw another rectangle – same size as the first – on top of the first, with no windows but with an unseen staircase between it and the first floor. Label the second floor *Emotional*. Lastly, let's draw a triangle whose base spans just past either side of the second floor rectangle, to represent a third floor and roof. Label the third floor *Cognitive*. Now, let's bring some life into our house.

Rather than starting on the first floor, let's go all the way to the very top and start with the top, or *cognitive* floor of our human condition house. Remember, this model works for everyone with average or higher mental faculties. Here we find the highest level or order of our actual being or self. This is where we formulate, store and access our beliefs, preferences, values, thoughts, ideas, and memories. This is also where we make decisions about each of these throughout every day... while we're conscious. Granted, some of our beliefs, preferences and values are predisposed by genetics (inherited), while many are the result of our exposure to our environment. The most powerful activity that occurs in this dimension is decision-making.

The second, or *emotional* floor is where we maintain our biases, partialities, and feelings about our third floor inventory *(beliefs, preferences, values, thoughts, ideas, and memories)*. This is where we *internalize* and *experience* things in life. We tend to rate or rank these experiences on a scale involving two polar opposites: *extreme pleasure,* and *extreme displeasure or pain,* respectively. As we experience life, our perception of these events are instantaneously – and subconsciously at times – compared and contrasted with similar past experiences... those memories we store on the third floor. So, if we have a similar memory of a past event, and if that memory was pleasant to us, then we tend to approach the new event with a more open embrace. The more pleasurable the memory of the experience, the less guarded or apprehensive we are. Conversely, memories of unpleasant or painful experiences, tend to cause us to be more cautious as we proceed toward and through the current, similar event. But, sometimes, we either don't pay attention to these memories or we just *short-circuit* (ignore) them, and hope and pray for a different outcome. As our powerful mind is making decisions all day, our emotions are tugging at or pushing/pulling in different directions to persuade our ultimate decisions. So, why do we ignore our memories sometimes? Why do we make choices and decisions that we should *know better*? My belief is because there is some form of reward that we're associating with that decision. Maybe it's the risk of it all… that MAYBE, just maybe it'll turn out differently or better this time. The point being that, even with the tug-of-war that is playing out constantly between our cognitive and emotional dimensions, what we choose will ultimately effect the outcome… every time. I see our emotional dimension as a two-way filter between our cognitive and behavioral dimensions, that can, and does, have an extraordinary impact on our lives through our experiences with others.

Last but not least, we arrive on our first, or *behavioral*, floor. Here we find the sole tool we use for interrelating and communicating with others, every day. This is how we go about interacting with others, giving and getting what we want and need to and from others. Our behavior is the result or reflection of the outcome of the tug-of-war between our cognitive and emotional dimensions. Our behavior manifests in any one or combination of three forms: : *verbal, paraverbal,* and *nonverbal. Verbal* behavior includes spoken or sung words, sentences, phrases, paragraphs, stories, etc. that involve the use of our voice or speech. *Paraverbal* behavior includes sounds that we make that do not involve the use of words, sentences, phrases, paragraphs, etc. Some examples of paraverbal behavior are: cries, laughter, clapping our hands, moans, sighs, screams, and non-vocal music. Nonverbal behavior includes all other behavior that does not involve verbal or paraverbal behavior, such as writing, texting, sign language, facial expressions, postures, and gestures. So, we can assert that behavior and communication, respective to the human condition, are synonymous and the vast majority of our behavior is chosen.

As a representation of the *human condition*, and using the three-floor house model for illustration purposes, most of us spend the majority of our time moving (consciously and subconsciously) between all three dimensions throughout the course of every day. This constant oscillation of decision-making is a wonder of the human mind that serves to protect, nurture and preserve us. So, you see, our human condition stays pretty busy every day all day. That's why we say we're fresher or think more clearly in the morning (or right after we awaken), and that we're *worn out* or *foggy* at the end of the day. All three dimensions of our condition are tired and tried. It's time to rest all three, so we can start all over tomorrow.

This is my illustration of the three-floor or dimension *Human Condition* and *Conflict House* model *(fig. 1)*. As you can see, this model also represents the dimensions that comprise our *conflict condition.* Keep the different levels of accessibility in mind as we move through the Lessons of this Module.

Figure 1. Human Condition and Conflict House Model

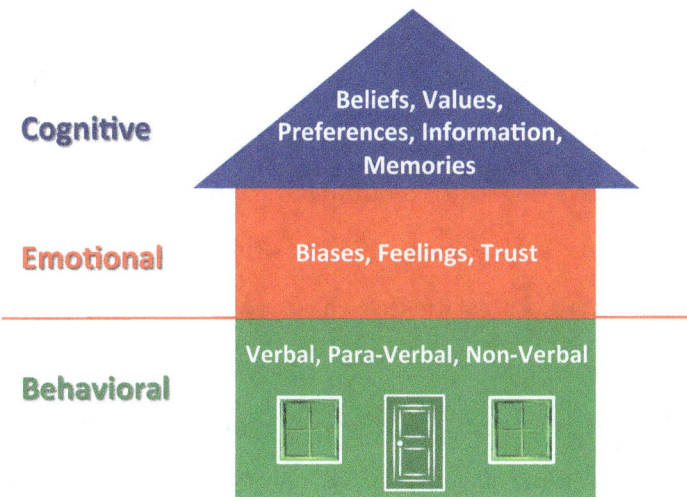

Let's examine each of these dimensions in greater detail so you have a more thorough understanding of the origins of all human conflict.

The Cognitive Dimension.

I'll begin at the top of the house, with the third floor, for reasons that will make perfect sense once you have completed all of the Lessons in this Module.

The cognitive dimension is the highest order of the three because this is where we process thoughts and ideas and make decisions. As rudimentary as this seems, it is only as complicated as it needs to be for the purposes of this Module. Here, we develop and store our *beliefs, values, and preferences…* all products of our thoughts, ideas, perceptions, experiences, and memories. Everything in this dimension has been saved and stored here for a variety of reasons and can only be accessed by that person. No one else will ever know what is really in our cognitive dimension, and we ourselves will likely never know everything that is within our own cognitive dimension. Some of the contents of our cognitive dimension are genetic predispositions and some are acquisitions. Let's take a closer look at the main categories of these contents: *beliefs, values, and preferences.*

Beliefs are the strongest element of our cognitive dimension as these are the "yes" or "no" decisions we have made in our lives. What we *do* believe and what we *do not* believe. There's no grey area about our beliefs… nothing wishy-washy. So, what are some of the things you believe in or believe to be true? These are questions that will only be answered "*Absolutely!*" or "*Absolutely NOT!*" (emphasis added). We usually identify our beliefs most easily with religion, close relationships and science. For example, if you are a devout Jew, Christian, Buddhist, or Muslim one would likely consider this to be your religious *faith* or *belief*. Why you share this belief is generally going to be most heavily persuaded by your exposure to your external environment - the most influential people in your life. If you believe that another person loves you (to any extent) or genuinely has your best interest in mind or would never cause you pain, it is because you trust or believe that person's intentions toward you. Lastly, if you believe the sun will rise in the east tomorrow morning, and set in the west in the evening, or you believe that one gallon is 128 ounces, or you believe that a mile is 5,280 feet then one would assume that you believe in science, technology, engineering and/or math. You either believe it or you don't.

Values are another thing altogether. So, let's use you as an example. What do you value? Remember, it can't be anything you believe or prefer. Most people will say they value their life, the lives of others. They value their family and the relationships that comprise their family. They value their freedom and they value that they get to enjoy it every day. They value being rested and taking good care of themselves and their health. They value individual relationships for a variety of individual reasons. Answer the question honestly. What do you value, and why do you value it?

Our *preferences* are precisely where our lives get personal and intimate, all day every day. Our preferences are like our own private little island or wilderness camp in the most beautiful part of the world where it's all about us. What are your preferences? Chocolate, vanilla, strawberry? Blue jeans or a suit? Tennis shoes or flip-flops? Fish or steak? Mountains or white sandy beaches? Bologna or peanut butter sandwich? Veggies or Jelly Beans? Deep sea fishing or reading a book inside? Sugar or artificial sweetener or no sweetener at all? Interstate or back roads? Creativity or predictability? Certainty or uncertainty? Scary movies, romantic movies, or both? The list goes on and on and on and on. Here's a twist for you… your preferences aren't just what you like the most, they are also what you dislike the most and the order you rank everything in between.

In our cognitive dimension, our beliefs, values and preferences are largely a result of a voluntary decision we've made, or one we will make in the future. Did your religion choose you or did/do you choose what to believe? Are you required to value your family or did/do you choose to value them? Is it mandatory that you eat a certain food, or do you choose what you eat? So, you see, our individual power or locus of control isn't in decision-making alone. It is, however, in understanding the power of the individual, voluntary decisions we make all day, every day.

So, what influences our decisions so much? Why do we make some great decisions, and other times we make some really stupid decisions? How random is what happens to us in our lives? Time for more relief… what influences our choices and decisions most ranges from extreme pleasure to extreme pain. Let that soak in for little while.

The Emotional Dimension.

Our *emotions* work in tandem with our *cognition*, simultaneously weighing risk against reward, pain against pleasure. How we *feel* - physically and mentally - in these situations develops our biases toward and against whether we want to repeat an experience. Remember, we're not necessarily choosing risk over reward, or pleasure over pain... or vice versa. Sometimes we choose based on comparative value... *Is the risk worth the reward?* or, *Is the reward worth the risk?* When's the last time you made a choice based on the comparative value of your options? Maybe it was whether to take the straight or scenic route to work today. Was it whether to get gas in your car last night on your way home, or to wait and get it in the morning on your way to work? Which option has the higher value to risk ratio?

Our emotions serve us in the role of biases and impact our behavior *(verbal, paraverbal, nonverbal)* more than our beliefs, values, and preferences. How we *feel* about our beliefs, values, and preferences has the most direct and profound impact on our behavior. To be clear, we have two types of feelings: tactile feelings (touch); and, emotional feelings (physiological). Our physiological feelings are when our emotions intersect with our cognition. So, when we say *our feelings are hurt* we mean that someone has offended us as a result of how we interpret some form of their behavior. It is possible for our feelings to be hurt inadvertently by another person for a variety of reasons. Sometimes, a person simply may not know that another takes offense or exception to a certain behavior of theirs. In a group or mob, it is more likely that a person can and will offend a complete stranger without ever meeting them. So, the status quo idea that someone's beliefs, values or preferences offend someone else, or their feelings is a complete misconception because we don't, and never will, know what anyone else *(other than ourselves)* believes, values, prefers, or feels. We only know what they demonstrate to us through their behavior.

Because our emotions are triggered by the verbal, paraverbal or nonverbal behavior of others, we have an opportunity to gain some control over the impact of their behavior. For example, how does it make you feel when someone tells you how smart you are? How about when they adamantly agree with something you say or believe? How about when they adamantly disagree with something you say or believe? What about when they adamantly and passionately tell you that your beliefs are completely wrong? And... what about if they are rude and vulgar when they adamantly and passionately tell you that your beliefs are completely wrong? Our range of feelings - *from positive to negative* - vary based on this dichotomy. Think of how many times a day you disagree with someone, anyone. Now think of how many times someone disagreed with you today. In each scenario, how did that affect your emotional feelings? Now consider the moment in each scenario when you had the opportunity to change your emotional response/reaction. To be able to exercise control over your emotional response/reaction is a great demonstration of first person power.

That said, it is impossible for anything other than one's behavior to affect the emotions of another, and the latter has a choice as to how their emotions are affected. In other words, if someone hurts me *physically*, I don't have a choice as to whether that hurts me *physically*. If someone's behavior is otherwise offensive to me, it is ultimately my decision whether or not my *emotional feelings* are hurt. That may be a tough concept for you to embrace, but hang in there, this will come full circle by the end of this Module.

So, rest easy knowing that it isn't true that we have absolute control over what bothers or offends us. Nor is it true that we have absolute control over how we respond or react when something or someone bothers or offends us. What is true is that we generally exercise a *fraction* of the control or power we have, and are capable of, when it comes to how and if we respond to our feelings. In no way am I suggesting that we internalize everything and hope to not explode later... I'm suggesting no such thing. What I am suggesting is that IF we choose to explore our abilities to exert control and power over our responsive behavior, and IF we choose to exercise and develop these abilities, we can and will have more responsive and reactive behavioral control and power than ever before, and probably more than most everyone else in our lives.

So, how about putting this to the test? Pick a routine scenario that occurs regularly in your life - one that gets on your nerves almost every time it happens. For me, it's driving in Nashville traffic. It doesn't matter if it's on the Interstate or a back road. It doesn't matter where I am, where I'm going, what I'm driving, the time of day, or the weather conditions. I will encounter the most inconsiderate drivers on the face of Planet Earth. Guaranteed. So, what's yours? In my *driving in Nashville* example, the reality is that I have SEVERAL choices and decisions to make that will directly impact my *experience*. Pause... I want you to begin thinking about *experience - your experience* in the scenario. The choices I have include *(but may not be limited to)* taking one of a few different routes, leaving earlier than usual, taking a cab, taking a bus, calling Uber or Lyft, getting gas the night before or waiting to the morning of my commute. Next, based on the choices I believe that I have, I **WILL** make a decision or two from these choices. What's that? What if I don't do anything? What if I just stay home and don't go at all? Well, guess what… that's a decision too. It's called avoidance, and avoidance is the Human Being's innate response to conflict. And guess what promotes avoidance more than anything. Our biases… our emotional biases. Dread, fear, regret, frustration, etc. and they all reside in our memories… our past. Past mistakes or misjudgments that we don't want to repeat because of some sort of displeasure or pain we *experienced*.

To emerge successfully from this Lesson, I want you to consider this philosophy, idea or *mantra* of mine: *"There is and never will be anything that has already occurred to me or others that I or they will ever be able to change, undo or redo. Never. My power and their power is right now and in my future and their future where no one of us has yet made a single choice or decision."* Feel free to write this down, stick it to the mirror in your bathroom, on your computer screen, wherever and recite it as often as you need to. Eventually, if you choose to allow yourself, you will begin to realize and experience this power and control of your emotion-driven responsive and reactive behavior.

So, it's all about understanding the power of choice and decision. After all, what other power do we have? Do you see the power of your decisions? Even the smallest of them? If you want to embrace this power, start right now. It's simple, really. The easiest place to start practicing your power is with your regrets. Everyone has regrets. What's your worst or most pressing, upsetting, or debilitating regret? Have you stopped confronting or discussing or *worrying* about it? If it's still a regret and you have pushed it out of view, you're really only avoiding it. If regrets are to be truly resolved, they have to be confronted.

Most regrets are big and/or messy - which is why we're avoiding them. So, take a deep breath *(do it now - you can thank me later)* because you don't have to resolve the regret right now… not all of it. Regrets are like the proverbial *elephant in the room* that we want to get out of the room, but because of the enormity of the elephant, the small size of the room and doors and windows, we can't begin to imagine that this elephant is going anywhere except against or on top of us. Sound familiar? So, what do we do? How do we begin to process this regret, or get this elephant out of the room, out of the house and out of our lives? I'm glad you asked.

Before you get ahead of me, I am not going to say anything about *cutting up the elephant*. For one, that's not the best approach for the elephant, the room or anyone in the room; two, I love elephants; and three, that would be very messy. You might be thinking that I'm trying to be funny right now, but I'm not. I want you to look at each of these reasons *(to not cut up the elephant)* as the metaphor they're intended. One, if we attempt to cut up the elephant - *the regret* - what have we accomplished? Have we minimized the regret? No, we haven't. We've only spread the regret into places we never intended *(under the couch, behind a table… yeah, more metaphors)*. Two, I'm not the only person that loves elephants… heck, I'd say most people *(with a heart)* love elephants. So, the biggest part of the elephant - *the regret* - represents someone or a group of people we love - which is why we have the regret. Because we are certain that we've hurt or betrayed them. Three, when we try to dismantle a regret, or convince ourselves that if we adequately address the most serious part of it, we don't have to worry about the rest. *The rest should just take care of itself.* That never works. Rather, the regret has many parts and we have to adequately address *each* of them. All of them… no matter how messy it makes us.

Time for some relief? Here it comes. Regret is the most damaging, pervasive, and prolific emotion humans experience. It saturates us. It smothers us. It consumes us. It splatters on those closest to us. It confines us until it eventually defines us… *if we choose to allow it.* In every case, it took two or more people to create this elephant/regret and it will take those same people to adequately address and resolve it.

But, I don't know what to say. I don't know where to start. Oh my gosh, they would never talk to me about this. I'm so embarrassed I can't contact them. They'll never forgive me, so what difference does it make? They'll never admit their part in all of this, so what difference does it make.

Each of these responses and/or reactions translates to *avoidance, avoidance, avoidance, avoidance, avoidance,* and *avoidance.*

What are we really avoiding? Are we avoiding a person or people? Are we avoiding the topic? Are we avoiding a place, a car, a house, an animal, food? No. None of that or anything else tangential you or anyone else could ever come up with. We're avoiding - or so we think - some sort of pain we fear. Real or imagined, all fear is real. What might create fear in some may not create fear in others. It's a different and special experience for each of us and no one else knows what the other is feeling or how this fear is impacting their lives. So, what do we do? What can we do about this or any fear? The answer rests *reliably* in one word - Stop. Stop avoiding the regret. Stop avoiding the people involved with you in the regret. Stop avoiding the fear of the pain that might come along with confronting the regret. Stop imagining pain into your life. Stop avoiding any shame or guilt that might haunt you. Choose to be brave. I promise, you can handle this. Just take it one step at a time. Make a plan to get that elephant out of your room and out of your house. Remember, destroying the elephant never works… it just makes a bigger mess. Maybe think of making the door wider, or taking down a wall long enough to get the elephant out. Otherwise, it isn't going anywhere.

The Behavioral Dimension.

To begin this lesson, let's take a look at a few of the most commonly accepted definitions of *behavior*.

Merriam-Webster Dictionary

noun

be·hav·ior \bi-'hā-vyər, bē-\
1. *a* : the manner of conducting oneself *criminal behavior normal adolescent behavior*
   b : anything that an organism does involving action and response to stimulation
   c : the response of an individual, group, or species to its environment *They are studying the behavior of elephants in the wild.*
2. the way in which someone conducts oneself: *We were grateful for the gracious behavior of our hostess. The children were rewarded for good behavior. Be on your best behavior.*; *also* : an instance of such behavior *unacceptable social behaviors*
3. the way in which something functions or operates *They tested the behavior of various metals under heat and pressure.*

Oxford English Dictionary

noun
mass noun
1. The way in which one acts or conducts oneself, especially towards others.
   '*he will vouch for her good behavior*'
   '*his insulting behavior towards me*'
   as modifier '*behavior patterns*'
   count noun '*management is a set of techniques and behaviours for getting things done*'

   1.1 The way in which an animal or person behaves in response to a particular situation or stimulus.
   '*the feeding behavior of predators*'

1.2 The way in which a machine or natural phenomenon works or functions.
'the erratic behavior of the old car'

American Psychological Association
The actions by which an organism adjusts to its environment.

So, why is this important? Why do you suppose I've offered *these* specific definitions of behavior? It's so we can see how competing resources agree - to a great and simple extent - as to what *behavior* is — academically, scientifically and practically.

But, of these definitions, and at least 10 others I found, not one of them defines behavior *practically*. So, what is a practical definition of behavior? Human behavior, specifically. Based on my experience as a conflict resolution practitioner and expert - and in the context of intra-, inter- and extra-personal conflict - I define *human behavior* similarly to an amalgamation of those I've cited above. Additionally, I divide the practical definition of behavior into four distinct segments: *verbal* behavior, *paraverbal* behavior, *nonverbal* behavior, and a *hybrid* of any/all of these three.

What purpose does behavior serve humans? Why do we talk? Why do we make sounds and noises *(laughter, cries, screams, melodies)*? Why do we posture, gesture, signal and micro-signal through our movements? Behavior serves humans *(and other species of animals)* as our sole means of communication with one another. So, I would assert that among humans, behavior and communication are synonymous and inextricably linked and that we communicate in the exact same fashion as we behave: verbally, paraverbally and nonverbally.

So, why do we communicate with each other? The simple answer is to meet our wants and needs. If someone has something, or has control of something we want or need, we will - in one or more of three ways - communicate that to them. We may *tell them* or *say* or even *sing* what we want or need (verbal: includes sounds and words). We may *sigh, moan, grunt, cry, laugh,* or *groan* to indicate what we want or need (paraverbal: includes sounds and noises only – no words). Or, we may simply point, write a note, send a text message, or just take what we want or need (nonverbal: includes gestures, writing, physical behavior without words or sounds/noises) without the other person's knowledge or permission. In any case, we have communicated a want or need. *What* we want or need.

To help us have a better understanding of human behavior let's discuss *how* we communicate our message to others. How effectively do we convey the urgency or importance or priority of the want or need? How convincing and influential *are we actually* compared to how convincing/influential *we want to be*, compared to how convincing/influential *we think we are*? And... what is influencing our behavior the entire time we're attempting to convince or influence someone else about our wants or needs?

To say there's a lot at work in these types of scenarios would be a huge understatement. But, a quick review of everything we covered in the previous Lessons on our *Cognitive* and *Emotional Dimensions* tells us what we need to know. Our wants and needs are based on our beliefs, values, and preferences, filtered through our biases, and our physiologic experiences - or what we like and dislike based on the experiences we had.

For example, if I really enjoyed going deep-sea fishing *(for any variety of reasons)*, I would probably want to go deep sea fishing again, primarily because I enjoyed it. I might adamantly refuse to eat liver and onions because of an experience in my past that wasn't pleasant, or was very bad *(maybe I got sick and never forgot the details of that experience)*. So, to say that *we do what we like to do because we like it* and *we don't do what we don't like to do because we don't like it* might seem a bit confounding, but they're very accurate points just the same. Look at it this way, if you could live the rest of your life doing only what you love to do, would you jump at that opportunity? Of course you would, but what's the reality?

The reality is that we all have to do a lot of things that we don't love, don't like, dislike and even hate every day. Right?

How many different things do you do each day that are purely by choice? How many of them do you really not like doing? Hate? Now, think of a thing or two that you do frequently that you really don't like to do - or hate to do. Why do you do them? For the broad range of answers you might have to this question, there is one central and reliable reason every time. It's because there is some form of value or reward to you in doing it. For example, if you really dislike your job but you get up and go to work each day... why do you do it? Need the money perhaps? In a broader but simpler sense, we do these things because they solve some sort of problem, need, or want we have. You might even say that they help resolve some of your conflicts.

Ultimately, our behavior is dominated and driven by the power we exercise over our choices and decisions. If we can do so many things each day that we don't like, then why does it seem so difficult to manage other choices and decisions in our lives? I say it's because we are human beings and we don't live in a static condition. Everything around us is in a constant state of change - and so are we, whether or not we want to or agree.

So, these three dimensions *(cognitive, emotional, behavioral)* not only define and diagram where conflict comes from, what causes it to arise, and create such havoc in our lives, they also give us the answers for how to manage and resolve our intra-, inter-, and extrapersonal conflict:

- Because I used to have a hard time *explaining* this whole idea of conflict in the three-dimensional human, I decided to *describe* it instead. That's what we'll cover in Chapter 3: PIpCC. *The Phillips Interpersonal Conflict Condition model.*

3. PIpCC

So, you might be wondering why I'm just now describing all of this to you instead of starting in Lesson 1 of Module 1. If you are, it's because, over time, I've learned that if description is used ahead of explanation *(in any learning setting)*, the learner tends to lose interest and starts filling in their own blanks or skipping several blanks altogether.

In this Chapter, we'll explore the model I created to illustrate, demonstrate, and describe what we look like in our day-to-day interactions and conflict with one another as three-dimensional beings. Or, our interpersonal conflict condition. Remember those three dimensions? Free reminder: *cognitive, emotional, and behavioral.* We're going to look at this model in terms of *triangles, spheres,* and *blobs.* What they are and which describes you best. Which describes me best. Which describes others best. Intrigued yet? Keep reading.

Triangles.

What do we know about triangles? They have three sides. They have three inner angles and three outer angles. What else? Well, all we're going to be concerned about is their three sides.

First, let's visualize ourselves – each of us – represented by triangles. I'm a triangle, you're a triangle, everyone's a triangle. Any guesses what the three sides of our triangles are? I'll give you until you finish reading this sentence to think about it. OK, I'll tell you. They represent the three dimensions of our *interpersonal conflict condition: cognitive, emotional, and behavioral.*

In my original Simple Individual Model *(fig. 2.)*, I rationalized that each of the sides of the triangle represented one of the three dimensions of our inter-personal conflict condition.

Figure 2. Simple Individual Model

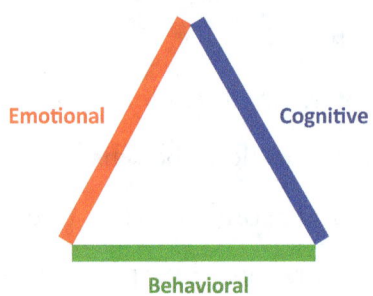

The location of each of the sides/dimensions of the triangle isn't as relevant as the fact that each side/dimension of our conflict condition remains in contact with the other two. In this model, my thought was that because we only share our behavioral dimension with others, it is the side of our triangle that we face toward the person or persons we're communicating with, as illustrated in my Simple Interpersonal Model *(fig. 3.)*.

Figure 3. Simple Interpersonal Model

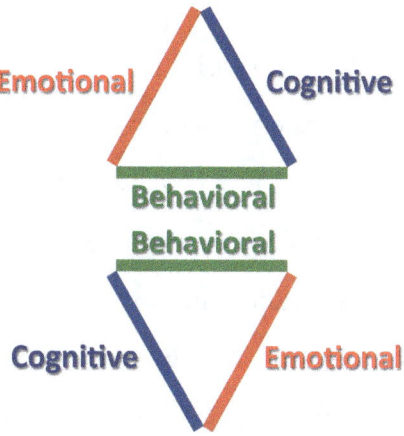

As I began to consider this model more deeply and began to think of group conversations, I imagined each person situated in a fashion where the *behavioral dimension* of everyone in a simple group *(fig. 4.)* of three people was facing the others demonstrating their focus on, and attention to the conversation or discussion.

Figure 4. Simple Group Model

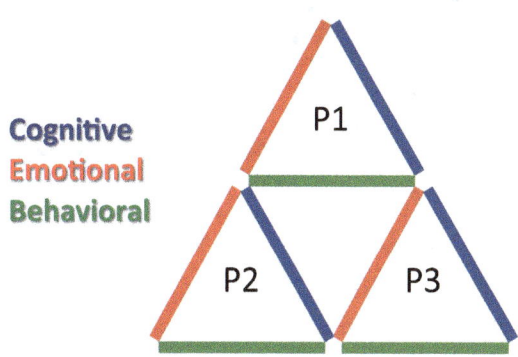

As this idea grew, so did the different formations of different number of people in as many group formations I could imagine. Like the Simple Meeting Model *(fig. 5.)*, used to illustrate the attention and focus of the group on a common task(s); or the Simple Conference Model *(fig. 6.)*, that illustrates a larger group of people focused on any variety of common tasks, interests or goals; or the Simple Classroom Model *(fig. 7.)* that illustrates a typical classroom or a basic military formation; or the Simple Seminar Model *(fig. 8.)*, that illustrates an open discussion and learning environment; or, the Random Crowd Model *(fig. 9.)*, that illustrates a simple rendition of crowd behavior comprised of simple individuals, simple inter-personal, simple group, and simple meeting models. This model could be representative of an after-hours get together, a family reunion, etc.

Figure 5. Simple Meeting Model

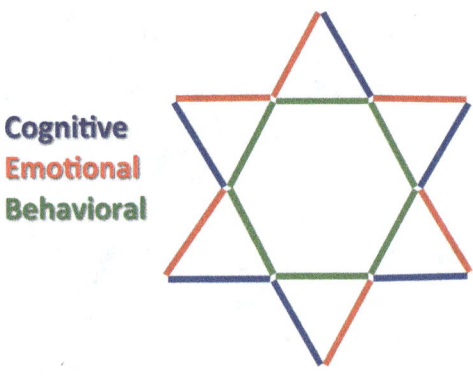

Figure 6. Simple Conference Model

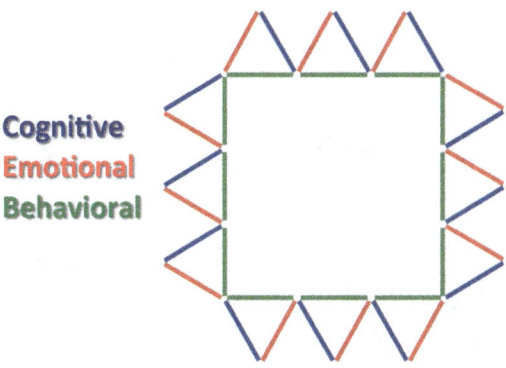

Figure 7. Simple Classroom Model

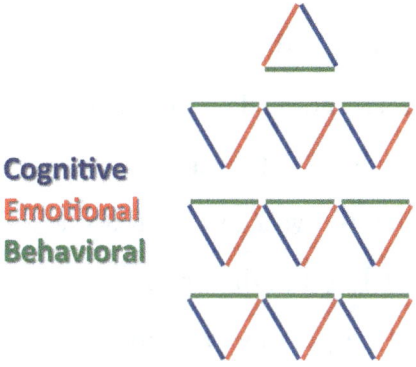

Figure 8. Simple Seminar Model

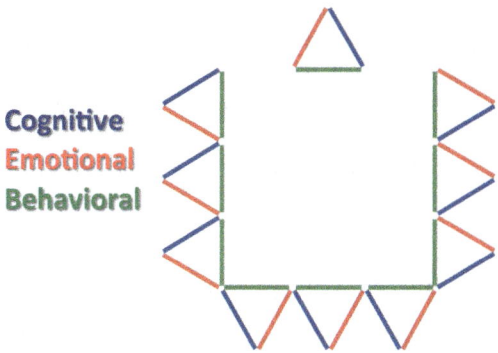

Figure 9. Random Crowd Model

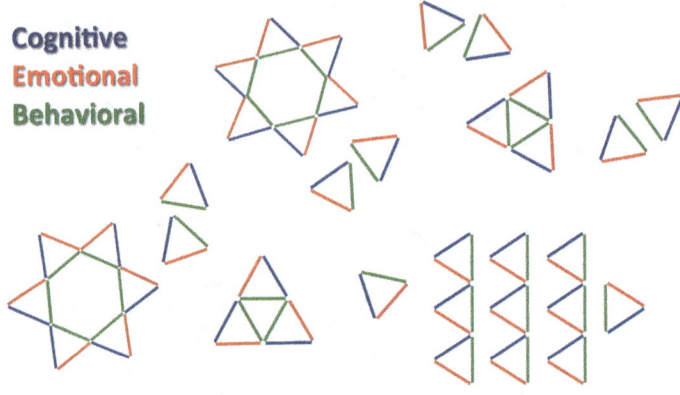

I began to notice a flaw in the Triangle model's theory after creating the Random Crowd Model *(fig. 9)* as I expected it to reflect individual, interpersonal and extrapersonal behavior adequately and accurately. What caused me to discover the flaw was greatly accidental but you can see it in the upper right corner of this model *(fig. 9)*. Look at the upper corner of the model and you'll see a Simple Interpersonal rendition… now look just down and to the left and you'll see what looks like a lop-sided, disconnect bowtie. See it? Once you find it, notice the direction of the green *(behavioral dimension)* sides of the two triangle. They're not focused entirely on one another, rather they seem to be perusing the crowd or are otherwise distracted. Then I noticed another "flaw" to my model in the lower left corner of the same model. You'll see another Simple Interpersonal rendition, and then just above it and to the left you'll see two individuals whose green *(behavioral dimension)* sides are perpendicular to each other. The original model suggests that when interpersonal communication occurs, each party has the other party's undivided attention. Of course, this doesn't reflect reality, because even when we're alone with another person we have distractions, or our mind might be on another topic at that very same time. This observation made me realize that *three-dimensional* isn't the same as *three-sided*. For example, the original model suggests that, if we were simply out of another person's physical range of focus/sight/attention, we would then be able to see their cognitive and/or emotional dimensions *(i.e. if we walk behind someone, whether they know we're there or not)*. Which isn't true at all. Even if we observe someone from behind or the side, or above or below them, we can only EVER observe their behavior. I have to say this was a major AH-HA! moment for me. I knew I had it! I just didn't know what *it* was yet. But, I would soon... very soon.

So, as I continued to manipulate this model, I realized that, not only are we not... we're dots. We're dots because: the behavioral dimension is all we can hear, see, touch, taste, or smell of each other, and that dimension is the ONLY one of the three that is ever exposed or ever can be exposed, to anyone other than ourselves. So, following my color scheme (blue = cognitive, red = emotional, and green = behavioral) I figured that we are a blue dot within a red dot within a green dot. Eureka! Version 2.0 of my model was born!

Dots... or not?

Dots. After completing my Interpersonal Conflict Condition Model *(versions 1.0 through 1.9)* and realizing that the triangle wasn't anywhere near the representation I wanted to achieve to adequately illustrate these three dimensions... I surmised that we were, in fact, dots - after I mistakenly thought we were *circles or rings*. The same premise and principles in the triangle model remain in the dot model, but our shape changed. In this new model *(fig. 10)* each of the lower orders is larger than, and encompasses the next higher order. In other words, the illustration below represents a cross-section showing the individual dimensions in their respective places. So, to address the flaws with the triangle model, we see that in the dot model, only the behavioral dimension *(green layer)* is observable by everyone other than the individual represented. The emotional dimension is contained within the behavioral dimension, and the cognitive dimension is contained within the emotional dimension.

Figure 10. Simple Dots Model

By comparison, we can see how much more dynamic the dot model is than the triangle model, which resulted from the two observations *(flaws)* noted in the triangle model. Where the triangle model is linear and rigid, the dot model is more fluid and is a clearer representation of the three dimensions of our personal conflict condition than is the triangle model *(fig. 11.)*. In the dot model, our behavior is the most dominant and conspicuous feature, as it is when we experience each other.

Figure 11. Dots / Triangle Comparison Model

Next, as we consider our other characteristics when we interact with others, we know we each have a focal point of input and output - our face, eyes, nose, ears and mouth. So, because we can only face one direction at a time, and are limited by our periphery, an input/output portal (represented by the green trapezoid) was added to the model *(fig. 12)*. In this model, the trapezoid represents our area of focus or engagement - where we're looking, the direction our attention is drawn, where our mind is engaged at that moment. This model also suggests that everything beyond the individual's periphery (blind spot) is very likely not something the individual is focused on or engaged with. The individual's level of awareness of what is in or happening within this blind spot varies with each individual.

Figure 12. Simple Dots Individual Engaged Model

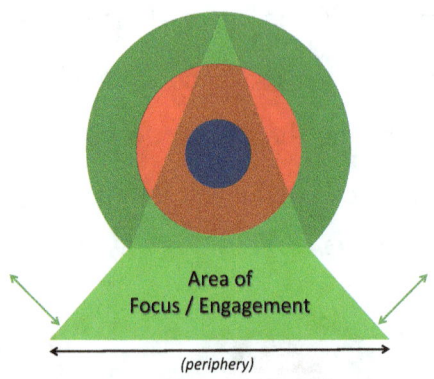

As we incorporate the interpersonal model, a few more interesting and key points arise. As I've illustrated below *(fig. 13.)*, we observe that each individual isn't static. In other words, when we interact with another person, we generally don't shut out the rest of the world and give them absolute 100% of our attention. We have other thoughts during every conversation. We're processing information at a rapid speed, making comparisons, trying to figure out the tidbits that are foreign or unclear to us, and we're making several decisions along the way. The green arrows on the outer corners of the trapezoid Area of Focus / Engagement (AFE) represent that oscillation in our attention and focus (distractions, etc.). Much of this is also represented by our physical movement *(shifting from foot to foot, turning or facing different*

directions, looking around, etc.). Next, in this dot model we can assert that the more parallel the individual's AFE is with the other's, the more likely it is that they are more deeply engaged and focused on the topic or task at hand.

Figure 13. Simple Dots Interpersonal Engaged Model

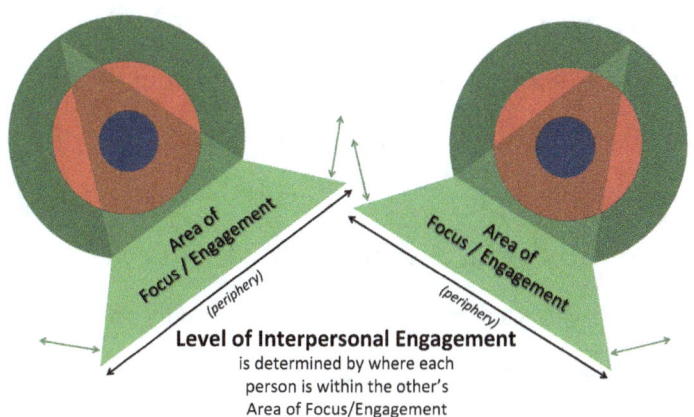

Now that we have an understanding of the human *conflict condition*, and a representative model of how we communicate and experience conflict with each other, let's take a look at the number one reason we experience interpersonal conflict and why: *personality differences*. We're all unique and no one else has the same personality as we do. Even identical twins - who share the exact same DNA - don't have the same personality.

Earlier in the book I discussed the different influences that effect and develop our beliefs, values, preferences, biases and our wide range of emotions, and how that we each experience each of them very differently. Each of these dimensions is also equally affected by our *individual biology* - or our genetic makeup and predispositions. Combined with our developed, or conditioned beliefs, values, preferences, biases, and emotional responses and reactions, our biology puts the finishing touch on what ultimately becomes what we refer to as our *personality*. In this context, our biology encompasses many of our physical, mental, and physiological traits that we cannot change *(aside from modern science and technology, of course)*: our race, our gender, our height, our eye color, our facial features, our hair texture, etc. Most of which are categorized as *physical traits*. While we may be able to have some of these traits scientifically or medically altered, we are still not changing our individual genetic code. Especially the genetic code that decides certain things about our personalities.

Multitudes of studies suggest and substantiate that our genetic code is also responsible for the individual traits that comprise our personalities. However, most inherited personality traits tend to be within the realm of mental health issues, or what is most commonly referred to as *chemical imbalances* and *neurotransmitter mis- and malfunction*. Many of these and related conditions are treatable with medicine and other rehabilitative measures... but not everyone has access to such care or simply "deal with it" in other ways... including avoidance. So, the moral of this story is that, as we will never really know another person's beliefs, values, biases preferences, and feelings, we will more than likely never know the medical/mental health of anyone outside of those in our inner-most circle. This should give us at least a snapshot of the individual *personality soup* we each bring to our relationships with others. Knowing this, it has been my belief and practice to stay acutely aware of all the complexities of our individual differences and the impact they have on our relationships.

While no mediator *(even if they are also a mental health professional)* should ever diagnose a mental or personality disorder of any party to mediation, they should always strategize to understand personalities and personality differences. That said the mediator, while staying focused on objectivity and neutrality, must pay close attention to the balance of each party's behavior. Is the party's behavior balance healthy and likely to contribute to a productive mediation session, or are they exhibiting *hyper* or *hypo emotion*-driven behavior, or are they exhibiting *hyper* or *hypo logic-* or *cognition*-driven behavior?

The next series of figures and commentary illustrate and address the strategy I have used over many years and hundreds of mediation cases, respective to the parties personalities and behavior at mediation. For my part, I give every party and every attorney the benefit of a doubt as to their ability and willingness to observe proper decorum at mediation. I take it a step further than just a handful of kind words, though. I begin each mediation by assuming each party and attorney will display *balanced and appropriate behavior.* Below *(fig. 14a.)*, I have illustrated a model representing how I see this balance, as it should appear. Then, as mediation commences, I graciously allow the parties and the attorneys to move their dots as the situation changes and requires. All the while, I'm looking for extreme changes in their behavior, being careful to not escalate or exacerbate someone that is agitated or about to become agitated.

Figure 14a. Simple Dots Balanced Individual Model

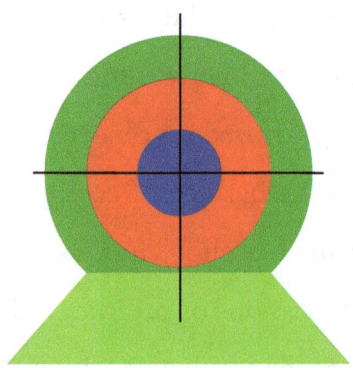

Mind you, while I have been a practitioner and student of conflict resolution for more than a decade - I'm not a mental health professional and am not qualified to diagnose a personality disorder or any other health condition for that matter, so I don't. I have, however, learned to *believe my eyes and doubt my ears* as it pertains to observation of human behavior. Because it is part of our nature to defend what is ours and to be as persuasive as possible to get what we want, I am fully aware of how persuasion can also be seen as deception. The great news for mediators is that

- as I say often - and turn heads and furrow brows simultaneously - mediation isn't about the truth... finding it, deciding it, assigning it, or awarding it. Honesty, and mutual respect, on the other hand, are paramount elements to every successful mediation. That said I expect the parties and the attorneys to be *persuasive* and even *deceptive* with me... because they want to get what they want.

So, here we are back at behavior and understanding everything that can possibly impact a person's behavior under any given circumstance. Here's more great news for the mediator - we're not diagnosing anything or anyone. Best news of all - the mediator will only spend a few hours or maybe one full day at mediation with the parties. The mediator's responsibilities and decision-making are confined to conducting the mediation process.

So, what are some of these personality traits the mediator needs to look out for at mediation? And how do you work with them? As you'll see in the next illustration *(fig. 14b.)*, I've used the same model as above on the left margin and labeled it below as "Balanced". The other characteristics depicted represent models of behavioral conditions I observe at mediation routinely, and they are imposed on my *dot model (fig. 14b.)*. For example, considering that the *trapezoid* in the model represents the general direction the subject is facing while gaining or giving information, our cognitive dimension moves about within our emotional dimension as we converse with and observe others, and our emotional dimension is moving about within our behavioral dimension. This model suggests primarily that the condition of our cognition, emotion, and behavior are not static, and that the position of the cognitive and emotional dimensions relevant to our physical behavior outlet determines our individual observable behavior.

For example, the *Hyper-Emotional* individual model exhibits emotion-driven behavior, the *Hypo-Emotional* and *Hypo-Cognitive* individual models exhibit more passive or reclusive/withdrawn behavior, and the *Hyper-Cognitive* model exhibits assertive/aggressive behavior.

Figure 14b. Simple Dots Individual Balanced/Imbalanced Model

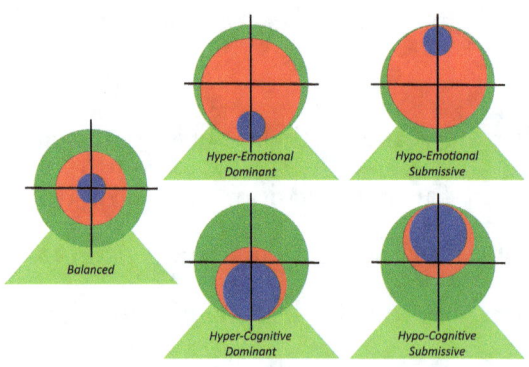

Further, this model suggests that each of the dimensions can change in proportionate *size* indicating that our cognitive and emotional dimensions can *increase* to practically the same size as our behavioral dimension, or decrease to non-existent. In such scenarios, for example, an *increased or inflamed* emotional dimension would likely cause erratic and aggressive observable behavior. In this same scenario, if the emotional dimension increases/inflames and the cognitive dimension decreases, the observable behavior will likely be even more erratic, aggressive and even violent. In scenarios where the model illustrates a disproportionately increased/inflamed cognitive dimension, the observable behavior would manifest as highly logical, process-driven and assertive. We'll discuss this in further detail later in the book.

But, wouldn't you know... after studying the new dot model a little while, I wasn't happy, again. Something was missing... something just wasn't right or complete about the model. What was it? I twisted and turned and flipped the model and then it hit me. The design or shape I was looking for wasn't a dot... it was a sphere. A sphere that not only illustrates height and width, but also depth. So, I changed the model to a sphere. Here's what it looks like *(fig. 15.)*. As you can see, the sphere model is only a slight modification of the dot model.

Figure 15. Simple Spheres/Dots Model

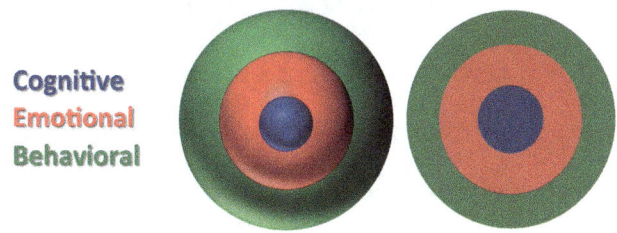

Better yet, I've shared a couple more perspectives *(figs. 16a. and 16b.)* that help demonstrate a deeper look into our conflict condition. We can see very clearly that this model *(fig. 16a.)* more effectively illustrates the three-dimensional characteristics *(height, width, and depth)* of each of the human conflict condition dimensions, and better demonstrates their relationships. In this example, the sphere or ball suggests that the object is movable. Movable, in fact, in any/every direction, which is representative of our ever-changing condition, whereabouts, mode, mood, etc. In this illustration we can easily see the structure of and relationship between the cognitive, emotional and behavioral dimensions of our conflict condition. When we close the sphere completely, the only dimension visible to the outside world is the behavioral.

Figure 16a. Simple Sphere Engaged Model

When we view a translucent version of the sphere model *(fig. 16b.)*, we get an external-to-internal perspective of the entire *balanced* conflict condition the model is intended to represent. We see that, regardless our external point of reference or perspective, we still only see the individual's behavior. Not their emotions, and not their cognition. Never. We can also see that, as information is gained and given, it is moving back and forth and through each dimension of the conflict condition suggesting that the information is being *processed through* the individual's biases (emotional dimension), *arriving at* the logic center (cognitive dimension) and essential *returning through* the biases and behavior to manifest a response or reaction to the stimuli. This activity is continuous and in rapid succession the entire time we are in a conscious state. The small green arrows to the upper left and upper right of the outermost corners of the AFE represent the oscillation or physical movement of the individual as they think, observe their surroundings, and interact and communicate with others. This version of the model very accurately illustrates the complete conflict condition.

Figure 16b. Simple Sphere Cutaway Model

Like the *dot model*, the sphere model illustrates the interrelation between each of the three dimensions of the human conflict condition, the critical addition of the perception of depth. In the rendition of simple interpersonal engagement below *(fig. 17.)*, we can see how the depth of the sphere model adds an element of activity or movement representative of two individuals sharing space and/or communicating. So, changing the model from dots to spheres was absolutely the right thing to do.

Figure 17. Simple Sphere Interpersonal Engaged Model

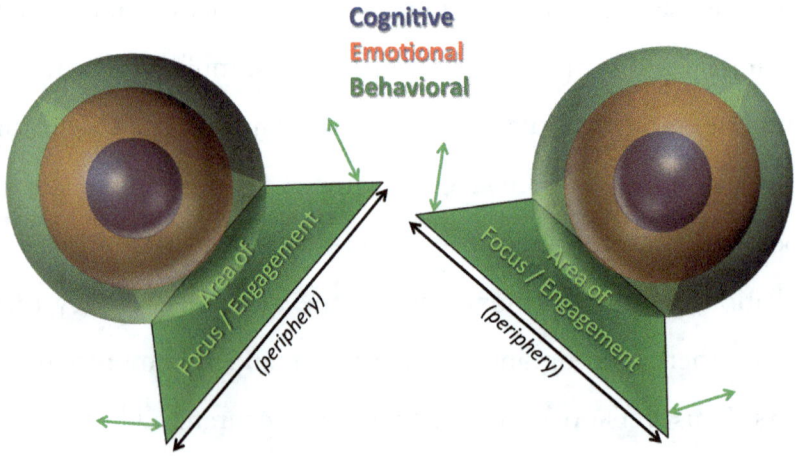

As the old saying goes, *"all good things must come to an end."* Or, in this case *revised*… again. Yep, I noticed another basic flaw to the model.

Blobs.

So, the *triangle model* is one-dimensional, the *dot model* is two-dimensional, and the *sphere model* is three-dimensional. So, what's the problem, you ask? Well, the problem with each of these models is that they are of perfectly proportionate shape *(square and/or round)*… and we humans are not. We're anything but. All three of these models suggest that we are mostly alike and our differences cognitive, emotional and behavioral differences can be easily measured and quantified. Wrong. Back to the drawing board. So, I walked away from all three models and decided to do my best to not think or write about this topic until and if I had a breakthrough. I did. About nine months later.

I was in an airport traveling for business and, while I was enjoying one of my most favorite pass-times - *people watching* - I commented to my co-worker about how many physical similarities we have but how creatively different each of our personalities is. I watched as some children played, some cried, some slept. I watched as some teenagers... well, most teenagers stayed in their own little worlds with their faces six inches from some device and their thumbs sliding all over it with some serious intent. I watched as some young adults *(I assumed were Millennials)* experimented as newlyweds and parents. I also observed how similar and how different some people looked that I *assumed* were related. As usual, I randomly commented that no matter if we're happy, sad, mad, ambivalent, whatever... we're each still a *big mess of different* compared to each other.

As I rationalized through this comment - I wasn't even thinking about the conflict condition model - I began to assign shapes to this mess. And then I said it. I said "We're like blobs... unique, individually, fairly predictable, and different blobs". That was it! That was the exact shape I was looking for *(fig. 18.)*. You see, the triangle, dots, and spheres are all symmetrical and uniform in shape, with our three conflict condition dimensions moving and changing size. That was the problem. Each of these dimensions - because they are a part of us - are also blobs. The emotional blob inside the behavioral blob and the cognitive blob inside the emotional blob. It made perfect sense!

Figure 18. Simple Blob Individual Model

As with the evolution of the triangle model to the dot model to the sphere model, the only thing about the premise of the model that changed is our *shape or interpersonal uniqueness*. Our conflict condition shapes are different because they represent our individuality - everything that comprises our individuality. Even the most minute or seemingly trivial things. Now, of course we can be and are very similar in many ways, but we are each so absolutely and completely unique. True one-of-a-kind souls and personalities… the different personalities that we experience with each other. Everything about every one of us is neatly encrypted and encoded in this big, beautiful blob we call self. In case you're wondering, there aren't any more shapes coming. Not as of the writing of this book, anyway.

So, I think you get the point at this juncture. We each handle things differently and that's okay. We think we know what others believe, think, value, prefer, feel… but we don't. We only know what they communicate to us through their observable behavior *(verbal, paraverbal, nonverbal)*.

I'm a blob… you're a blob… everyone's a blob *(fig. 19.)*. Who knew?

Figure 19. Simple Blob Interpersonal Model

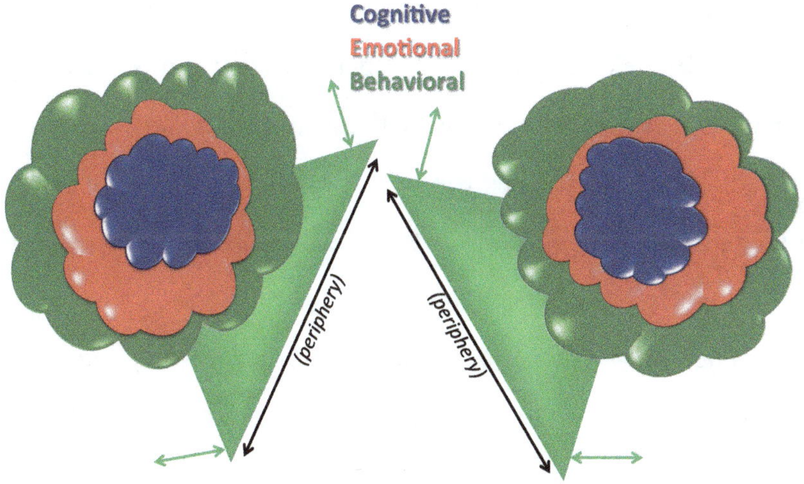

4. CONFLICT RESOLUTION & MEDIATION

Now that we're fully versed in where and how conflict arises, how it's exacerbated by our biases and feelings, and how it manifests in our behavior, let's examine how conflict is resolved. More specifically, the two approaches to interpersonal conflict resolution, *third party empowerment* and *disempowerment*, and the different *methods* of each approach.

The *empowerment* approach to interpersonal conflict resolution involves an informal, private, and confidential intervention by a neutral third party whose purpose is to facilitate discussions between the disputing parties that allow them to reach mutually acceptable agreements on the issues in dispute. Methods utilizing empowerment emphasize fairness, the needs and interests of the parties, procedural flexibility, balance of power and self-determination. *Mediation* and *Judicial*

Settlement Conference are the only two empowerment methods of interpersonal conflict resolution. Both encourage the parties to remain open-minded, think creatively and determine the outcome of their dispute, rather than allow it to be decided for them by one of the several methods of the disempowerment approach. In mediation, the neutral third party (mediator) has no decision-making authority. The same is true for Judicial Settlement Conference, but, because the neutral third party is a judicial officer, it is very likely that their background as a judicial officer will have a substantial impact on any settlement reached. Because of the judicial influence inherent to settlement conferences, mediation is the only true method of third party empowerment in interpersonal conflict resolution.

The *disempowerment* approach to interpersonal conflict resolution involves public hearings, depositions, trials, third party decision-making methods, and imposed outcomes. Each method of the disempowerment approach *(litigation, bench trial, jury trial, summary jury trial, arbitration, case evaluation, etc.)* places the parties at a distinct disadvantage by removing them from deciding the outcome of their dispute. In these disempowerment methods, the parties must simply accept what outcome or judgment is decided - no matter how unfavorable it may be. The outcome of interpersonal conflict subjected to any method of the disempowerment approach is based on one person's, or a small group of people's, perspective of the evidence that is presented in support of and against each party's position. Regardless the method of interpersonal conflict resolution, outcomes of disputes subjected to the disempowerment approach are inherently and extremely uncertain and unpredictable. Conversely, the outcomes of interpersonal conflict subjected to the empowerment approach are inherently more certain and predictable. When the power of the interpersonal conflict resolution rests and remains with the parties, the parties are much more likely to reach a mutually acceptable agreement, and an even greater number of those agreements remain intact.

In general, conflict or dispute resolution is as much a concept as it is an outcome-driven process. Often times, the *concept* of conflict resolution is overlooked because we tend to define it as an *event* whose outcome is an agreement or settlement. When we broaden our perspective and see conflict resolution as a concept, we see that it is a multi-faceted system of opportunities for the parties. For example, if we see our lives as a series of exercises in decision-making, we realize that our agenda is steeped in finding answers or solutions to questions and problems that relate to our needs and wants. So, we adopt a system of making decisions that best address or suit our needs and wants by embracing the concept conflict resolution on a moment-by-moment, situation-by-situation basis. Within this system of problem solving, we utilize a variety of skills-based methods to achieve the outcome.

The different *methods* of conflict resolution define the different practical approaches to the outcome. A *method* of conflict resolution is a well-defined process that has a distinct beginning point; a structured system of information gathering, analyzing, and comparing; an underlying decision-making element; an outcome finalization phase; and an ending point. Some of the best and most popular methods of conflict resolution in our court systems include: *litigation, arbitration, mediation, judicial settlement conference, mini trial, summary jury trials, and case evaluations.* While each of these methods is unique in its design and the process it utilizes to reach a final outcome or disposition of a dispute, they also share many common elements *(third-party disempowerment, adversarial, evidence-based, public accessible, non-private, non-confidential, protracted, and costly).*

For example, litigation, arbitration, mini trials, summary jury trials, and case evaluations are each evidence or proof dependent methods of conflict resolution. In each of these methods, once each of the opponents has presented evidence in support of their position, a third party *(judge, arbitrator, jury, case evaluator)* decides the outcome, based on their perspective of the persuasiveness of evidence presented. Because these methods are competitive by nature and design, and the parties do not get to participate in deciding the ultimate outcome, they are referred to as *third-party disempowerment* approaches to conflict resolution.

Judicial Settlement Conference operates more informally than these methods and is a hybrid of a judicial proceeding and mediation. This method of conflict resolution is presided over by a judicial officer *(judge, magistrate, referee, commissioner, special master)* who is in no other way involved in the dispute/case. This method is guided/directed by them based on the strengths and weaknesses of the opponents' respective positions, as perceived by the judicial officer. Depending on the personality of the presiding judicial officer, there will be varying degrees of third-party disempowerment throughout the judicial settlement conference. Remember, the judicial officer's *full-time job* is being a judge and making decisions on a multitude of lawsuits every day, so it can be challenging for them to change their role.

That brings us to *mediation*. Mediation is entirely unique compared to the other methods described above. Mediation is non-adversarial, private, confidential, expeditious, less costly, and decided by the parties - not their attorneys, not a judge, and not a jury. So, why is mediation so different than the majority of the other methods of court-based conflict resolution? Simply, it's because mediation is everything the other methods aren't. Primarily, because the mediator acts as a guide and facilitator to help the parties openly discuss their concerns and needs, and because the parties make all of the decisions about the final outcome of their case/conflict, mediation is the only *third-party empowerment* method of conflict resolution. Where the other methods aren't, mediation is based on the principles of:

- needs and interests of the parties
- fairness
- procedural flexibility
- privacy and confidentiality
- full disclosure
- self-determination

The three great tenets of the practice of mediation are *integrity, impartiality,* and *mutual respect*. We'll examine each more closely in the following lessons and gain a comprehensive understanding of how they work in concert to create mediation.

Integrity.

The most common theoretical hallmarks of *integrity* are honesty, honor, good character, probity, ethics, principle, morality, virtue, decency, trustworthiness, kindness, truthfulness, rectitude, fairness, sincerity, and scrupulousness. They are each theoretical in this context because no action is being demonstrated. So, how are each of these - *integrity* in particular - demonstrated? And how are they demonstrated by the mediator?

First, let's define integrity in the context of the mediation process and then in the role of the mediator.

In the context of mediation, integrity is defined by a common understanding that if mediation is to *work* - to serve the parties - then each of its elements *must* be bound by integrity. Integrity is demonstrated in mediation by the mediator's, the attorney's, and the parties' trust that: 1.) all parties will experience a fair and balanced opportunity to settle their dispute; 2.) everyone involved will remain honest, open and non-adversarial throughout the process; 3.) each party will be treated with respect and fairness, and allowed ample time to voice their concerns; 4.) the mediator is competent in their professional abilities as a mediator; 5.) the mediator will preside in a fashion that empowers the parties to make well-informed decisions with the advice of their attorneys; 6.) the only real obstacle to a settlement at mediation is the interests and intentions of the parties; 7.) the entire proceeding will remain private and confidential; 8.) the mediator may not be called as a witness in any related matter; and, that 9.) each party has an equal responsibility and accountability for a successful outcome.

While a lawsuit or a dispute may share many similarities with other actions, mediation must regard the *integrity of process* first by expressing no interest whatsoever in the terms of any agreement reached - or, the outcome of the mediation. The analogy I share with my students to demonstrate this is by imagining a sporting event, and that sporting event's venue or playing field. Let's use American football as an example. The well-groomed, well-prepared, properly marked, safe football field represents mediation. Prior to a game, a team of experts takes special care insuring that the field is *ready for game day*. They make sure the turf is the proper density and height, they make sure there are no holes or divots in the field that might cause an injury they make sure all boundaries and yard markers are properly demonstrated, and they make sure that both teams have adequate sideline amenities (benches, lockers, water stations, etc.). Now think about how theoretical it is to have a well-prepared football field that's never used. That's right... it only matters on game day when the teams take the field and the starting whistle blows. Until that time... what is it?

The other half of this analogy is the role of the mediator with respect to integrity, and the mediator themselves. The mediator's role is their position in the event *(mediation)* as the third party neutral that conducts discussions between the parties regarding their disputes - all the while maintaining fairness, balance, shared power, procedural flexibility, self-determination, mutual respect, presiding over and monitoring the entire process, arbitrating the ground rules, and deciding if the mediation process proceeds, and when it is concluded. This sounds a lot like the referee(s) at our football game, don't you think? So, the mediator job description is something else we'll find defined in the game rules. But, just like a well-prepared football field without a game is nothing more than a pretty, green field... the role of the mediator is purely theoretical until it's brought to life by the mediator, at mediation.

So, what does that look like? What does *mediator integrity* look like at mediation? During the football game, the referee isn't really interested in the score at all - except as to its accuracy. They are *very* concerned, however, with how ethically and safely each team member plays the game, the proper application of penalties if any rules are broken, and how much time is left on the game clock, and when the game is over *(when their job is done)*. Notice what I said about the referee's interest in the score. They have no interest in the score. That's not why they're there. If the field has been properly prepared, the players have been properly prepared and informed, then the only job of the referee is to ensure that the game is played as prescribed and agreed to, and to otherwise have no interest in the final score... rather only that each team *have the same opportunity* to play the game. Yeah, but what about how bad calls can affect the score of the game? What about when a referee lets one team get away with all kinds of penalties during the game? They're out there, and you know it! Well, that's the exact moment that the job description is being brought to life by an individual. Similarly, the mediator demonstrates integrity not just by what they do and what they don't do, but how they do it. We demonstrate integrity by demonstrating empathy, compassion, openness, honesty, transparency, non-avoidance, fairness, and competence equally among the parties and their attorneys. We demonstrate integrity at mediation by explaining the process and each party's role - before mediation begins. We demonstrate integrity at mediation by giving the parties a concise and clear overview of what will happen during mediation - how the process works - before mediation begins. Beyond that, we demonstrate integrity at mediation by keeping our word in fulfilling our role and permitting the parties to fulfill theirs, and by staying out of their way and allowing them to create an agreement that they find mutually acceptable.

In my experience, the biggest challenge the mediator faces at mediation is the urge to weigh the value of a particular settlement offer to one or both parties. It's not an easy thing to learn, but the sooner the mediator will and can learn to not care about the outcome of a mediation, the better. In other words, let the parties agree to whatever they want to agree to. As long as it isn't illegal, why would you care? If you do care, you might want to read this chapter again.

At mediation, the mediator must be the gold standard of integrity through an acute awareness of and accountability for their behavior.

Impartiality.

In the mediation profession we see words like *neutral/neutrality, equal/equality, fair/fairness,* and *good faith* used a great deal. While I see the point and purpose of these words, I disagree with their accuracy and proper use. The reality is that, as long as mediation is presided over by mediators and as long as mediator are humans, we are hardly capable of such lofty and unrealistic standards. The reason I nit-pick at these words is because *words matter at mediation.* The parties and their attorneys are at a heightened state of defensiveness and even anxiety many times, and as a result, pretty strong language is exchanged between the parties - language that's designed primarily to intimidate and defeat their opponent. So, the mediator must use great caution - and intent - to not add to this already fueled fire by carelessly using less than accurate wording.

First, let's deal with the *word* and *idea* of *neutral/neutrality*. Because we're human we have minds, and because we have minds we have beliefs, values, opinions, and preferences, and because we have beliefs, values, opinions, and preferences we have feelings that are ultimately reflected in our behavior. So, by definition, humans aren't capable of being neutral when it comes to interpersonal conflict intervention and resolution. It just isn't possible. But, what we are capable of is learning to be a little more *objective* every day in how we observe and react to events that occur to and around us. To otherwise think that we *can* be neutral is more than a lofty goal, it's an abundant waste of time. So, it's incumbent upon the mediator to make the realization early in their career (or as soon as possible, if you're not a newbie) that they *can* be objective with great practice, but *neutrality is unattainable.* At mediation, we set the tone, the tempo and the expectations of the parties *(considering that their attorneys have already set a tone of their own with them)*. You might be thinking that I'm mincing words, and you would be right. The reason I mince words like these is because if you say them, the parties hear them… and you don't get to define them for the parties. Even if you think you've defined them the parties are going to hear what they want to hear… so, choose your words very carefully because they're listening.

Next is *equal/equality*. Where do I begin? Well, what do you think of where you hear someone say something is equal or that equality is present/represented? What do you mean when you use these words? What do you think others mean when they use them? What do you think others think when you use them? See… this could go on forever. So, here's the point I'm making, equal/equality applies ONLY to mathematical formulas. It is a definite sum, product, quotient, difference, etc. and represents an absolute value. Something that doesn't apply in mediation. EXCEPT when we're talking about dollars and cents or the fair market value of a house or a boat. So, just don't use these words unless they are accurate in their intention and interpretation. What is the context? What is the fundamental meaning you want to convey? If it isn't the result of a mathematical formula, don't use *equal*. If you do, you're making a BIG assumption and that's not what mediator's do. So, "You know what I mean." is a phrase that should never come out of a mediator's mouth. Even in the Declaration of Independence - purportedly the most historic and profound proclamation every made - we read the immortal words **"We hold these truths to be self-evident, that *all men are created equal…*"** and then apply this to something that has resulted from our behavior as a child, teen, or adult when we compare the punishment that is assigned to that behavior. It isn't fair! I want equality! I'm guaranteed equality by being an American. But, how many people (including you) have read or can recite the rest of the phrase? Completed, it goes something like this: **"We hold these truths to be self-evident, that *all men are created equal, that they are endowed by their Creator with certain unalienable Rights, that among these are Life, Liberty and the pursuit of Happiness."** Well, how's that for some context? Equality applies here (in this pretty important document) to when we are born and that we are all born no more or less important than anyone else - not even because of the color of our skin, our gender, the affluence of our parents or grandparents, etc. It goes on to declare that we have equal Rights under God to live our lives, to live them free of government control and to be happy in everything we do, provided it doesn't infringe on these same Rights of others. As mediators we cannot be random, emotional *word slingers*. We must be intentional and strategic with every word we speak or write.

Next up, *fair/fairness*. Reminder, think *context*... it's all about context and you believing that words matter at mediation. When's the last time you heard someone say (maybe a co-worker, maybe a child, maybe yourself) "That's not fair!"? In most context, what does this really mean? Usually it means "That's not what I want!" or "That's not good enough!" or "They shouldn't get as good or better a deal than me!" or, here's my favorite, "I'm entitled to more/better!" Like the previous terms, I'm not suggesting that you leave this out of your vocabulary I am imploring you to use the word correctly, intentionally and strategically for the benefit of the mediation process.

So, what does fair/fairness REALLY look like at mediation? It's balance. That's all it is. As mediation progresses, the mediator should know that, to a great extent, they are starting at a point of significant imbalance between the parties for a variety of reasons. So, before rushing in to the negotiation and deal-making phase, the mediator must first establish as much balance with each party as they are willing to compromise. Only then, can or will the case settle. How do we achieve this balance, you ask? We do it by following the mediation process... every... single... time, all the time. We tell the parties who we are, what we're going to do, what *they're* going to do, what their lawyers are going to do at mediation, then we tell them how the process works... where we're going to start (*their* storytelling), what's next (*they* identify and prioritize the issues that need to be resolved), what's after that (we help *them* brainstorm to find out WHAT'S GOOD ENOUGH - to *them* - to settle each issue), what's next (write up and review the agreement, one issue at a time), and how we know when we're done (the entire agreement gets signed by them and the other party(s), everyone gets a copy of the agreement and everyone leaves). Did you notice how many times I said, "they" or "them" or "they're" or "their" or "THEM"? So, who is deciding what is and is not fair and to whom? The parties are deciding what is fair (GOOD ENOUGH) for themselves. So, in the context of mediation, fair/fairness should only be in reference to *value*.. the value to each party of getting their case settled at mediation that day.

And last... good old *good faith*. So, here's the most common misconception I hear at every mediation, at every mediation training seminar I hold, at every conflict resolution or conflict management class I teach... "The parties and their attorneys must participate in a settlement in good faith." OK, this one's really easy. Define it. Someone, please define good faith for me. Oh, I know we can each define what it means to us but unless a law, or Rule of Court, or Rules of Civil Procedure or some other authority defines good faith once and for all, we don't need to use it. Mediators... listen to me. Strike this short term from your vocabulary. These two words have caused some mediations to impasse, and some others to take much longer than they should have because they have a subjective connotation no matter how you use them (together). I don't use the term, but I often tell the parties that they have to participate in an honest and meaningful way while at mediation or we'll be wasting their time and money.

To bring it all home, the mediator must be prepared to address *rigid, confined, absolute language and behavior* at mediation as it occurs throughout the process. You're not going to be able to prevent or stop it, so you have to learn (want to learn) how to manage it as it happens. It helps if the mediator will see this behavior as defensiveness stemming from the amount of *uncertainty* the parties *aren't* willing to admit exists - that ultimately drives their fears and subsequent resistant behavior. I'm not saying the parties or their attorneys are in denial... what I am saying is that most (if not all) civil plaintiffs are completely unsophisticated about the litigation process - so they really have no idea what uncertainty awaits them at trial. Trial is all or nothing, basically. They really don't have a clue what they're in for. Their lawyer has probably tried to tell them this - amid the lawyer's declarations of how good they believe their case is - so this can be confusing to the parties. In domestic or juvenile cases, neither the plaintiff nor defendant - to a great, if not entire extent - knows what's happening or can happen at trial... and there isn't anyone that can talk them off of that "I want my day in court!" ledge either. By the same token, these same parties have no idea how much *certainty* is offered at mediation and how that certainty will empower them to genuinely get on with their lives. So, we mediators must inform them of it all... the good, the bad and the really, really bad (appeals, losing on appeal, etc.).

The mediator's ability to remain impartial will be tested throughout mediation by the things the parties say, how ridiculously the parties are behaving, and how inflexible they can be. The mediator must *weather the storm* and not allow the parties' or the attorneys' behavior to affect their impartiality. The parties and their attorneys are going to try to persuade you to see things their way in hopes that you'll work the other party over to their benefit. It's going to happen if it hasn't happened yet. Somewhere there is a mediation going on and in that mediation the parties and their attorneys are trying to persuade the mediator to help them get a better deal (whatever that means).

Lastly, partiality doesn't just refer to taking someone's side. It also implies that favoritism or bias is being shown *for or against* a party, issue or cause at mediation. So then, I can assert that mediator impartiality implies *freedom from favoritism or bias for or against a party, issue or cause at mediation.* We don't have a choice. This is what we do.

Mutual Respect.

In mediation, *mutual respect* is the glue that gets the agreements. Mutual respect is reciprocal and it is the mediator's responsibility to make sure that the parties know that this is not an option, but a mandate of the mediation process. So, let's break it down so you can break it down to the parties.

We know that *mutual* means reciprocal - everyone does it, no one gets a break - so let's be sure to understand what *respect* means at mediation. I'm sure this won't be surprising, but the meaning is no different than in any other context - except that we mediators are charged with instilling mutual respect in the mediation process, no if's, and's, or but's.

What we want the parties and attorneys to understand *primarily* is that mediation is like no other process or proceeding they have ever been, or will ever be, involved with. It is a process that is founded on the overt demonstration of respect for the parties and their dispute; that their case will not be treated like a number and it will not be paraded in the public eye for anyone and everyone to attend, at the cost of humiliation to the parties; that mediation is not and will not become adversarial at any time; that any agreement the parties may reach is their responsibility; and that no other person at mediation will tell them what they will and will not agree to, or otherwise do what is against their will.

With this knowledge and understanding, the mediator must then impress upon the parties the unique opportunity that they have at mediation. The unique opportunity to stop their lawsuit that day and get it off of their shoulders; to be finished with it once and for all, that day; to get some finality in their lives so they can move on, respectively, that day; to stop spending money on court costs and attorney's fees, that day; to enjoy the dignity of the privacy and confidentiality that only mediation can guarantee; to know that they can tell the mediator anything they want or feel they need to - knowing that the mediator cannot repeat a word of it to anyone without their permission; and to know, that they won't have to go to court again on this matter, ever.

So, how does the mediator communicate or demonstrate mutual respect and how do we demand it of the parties and their attorneys? Well, I have lots of good news for you. First, the mediator must *talk the talk* and *walk the walk*. The mediator can't be - or even appear to be - adversarial, ever. The mediator must always be and appear interested, considerate, empathetic, concerned, open-minded, creative and collaborative. We must be everything we want and expect them to be… and it won't be easy for anyone. Not even the mediator. So practice… every day of your life, wherever you are, whomever you're with. Always be and appear interested, considerate, empathetic, concerned, open-minded, creative, and collaborative. Seriously. In the grocery store, at the ballpark, at work, at home, at church, with your kids, with your in-laws/out-laws, with your neighbors, and friends.

Properly practiced, mutual respect isn't something you just do or demonstrate, it's something you become. Just like being a mediator isn't a switch you'll ever want to turn off and back on from time to time. Live your life as a mediator and through your life you'll be teaching others how to do it and that they can do it sooner and much easier than they realize. Live your life as a mediator and you'll give your spouse, your children, your friends, your family, your neighbors, your parishioners, your co-workers the best gift you can imagine. But first, you have to *decide* it's what you're going to do. Choose peace.

ABOUT THE AUTHOR

Clay Phillips is a mediator, mediator trainer, consultant, and professor of conflict resolution at two universities in his home city of Nashville, Tennessee. During his career, he has mediated more than 400 cases spanning a broad array of civil and domestic actions; he has trained more than 1,200 mediators, and is the author of ***The Mediator's Guidebook*** series on mediator and conflict resolution practitioner development. He also created the curriculum for a regionally accredited Master of Arts Degree in Conflict Resolution, which, to-date has more than 300 graduates. He holds a PhD in Business Administration *(Organizational Leadership Specialty)*, a Master of Business Administration and a Bachelor of Science in Business Management. He and his wife Deborah – and their fur baby Izzy – live just north of Nashville.

GET CONNECTED WITH CLAY

ClayPhillipsBooks.com
LinkedIn/in/ClayPhillips.com
@DrClayPhillips

www.ingramcontent.com/pod-product-compliance
Lightning Source LLC
Chambersburg PA
CBHW050544300426
44113CB00012B/2251